WORLD'S SCARIEST PLACES

HAUNTED HOUSES

ALIX WOOD

Gareth Stevens PUBLISHING

Please visit our website, **www.garethstevens.com**. For a free color catalog of all our high-quality books, call toll free 1-800-542-2595 or fax 1-877-542-2596.

Cataloging-in-Publication Data
Names: Wood, Alix.
Title: Haunted houses / Alix Wood.
Description: New York : Gareth Stevens, 2017. | Series: World's scariest places | Includes index.
Identifiers: ISBN 9781482459128 (pbk.) | ISBN 9781482459142 (library bound) |
ISBN 9781482459135 (6 pack)
Subjects: LCSH: Haunted houses--Juvenile literature.

First Edition

Published in 2017 by
Gareth Stevens Publishing
111 East 14th Street, Suite 349
New York, NY 10003

Produced for Gareth Stevens by Alix Wood Books
Designed by Alix Wood
Editor: Eloise Macgregor

Photo credits: Cover, 1, 3, 4, 13, 20, 25 © AdobeStock; 5 © Henry Gordon; 6 © Bidgee; 7 © Jane 2456; 8 © bvi4092; 9 © Tusela; 10-11 © Samantha Forbes; 12 © Arvid Karlsson; 14 © Dreamstime; 15 © Patrick Henry; 16 © Bob R. Richter; 17 top © D. Ramey Logan; 17 bottom © Urban Walnut; 18-19 © Asfandmajeed; 21 © Manfred Heyde; 22 © Dreamstime; 23 top © C.R. Botha; 23 bottom © Shutterstock; 24 © Rene Drivers; 26 © Harry Smith; 27 © Mark Grealish; 28-29, 29 top © Robert Knudsen; 29 middle © Alexander Gardner

Printed in China

CPSIA compliance information: Batch #CW17GS. For further information contact Gareth Stevens, New York, New York at 1-800-542-2595.

Contents

Whether you believe in ghosts or not, some houses have a really creepy **atmosphere**. A ghost is believed to be the spirit of a dead person. Ghosts are often said to **haunt** houses, especially houses where tragic deaths have occurred.

Even if you don't believe in ghosts, it's pretty easy to get scared in some of the world's most haunted houses!

THE SALLIE HOUSE, ATCHISON, KANSAS

The Sallie House in Kansas was a doctor's house. It is believed to be haunted by the ghost of a young girl named Sallie who died during an emergency operation there.

In haunted places, such as the Sallie House, people may feel strange sensations. They can feel like someone is there, even when the house is empty. They may feel a sudden drop in temperature, or hear mysterious noises.

Monte Cristo Homestead, Australia

Thought to be the most haunted house in Australia, Monte Cristo Homestead in Junee, New South Wales, has seen its share of chilling events. The Crawley family owned the house from when it was built in 1885 until 1948. During that time a maid fell to her death from the balcony, a young child died after being dropped down the stairs by the **nanny**, and a caretaker was shot when he opened the front door. The owners, Christopher and Elizabeth Crawley, are believed to still haunt the house, too.

A stable boy burned to death in his straw bed in the Monte Cristo stable. The boy had said he was too ill to work. His boss thought he was bluffing and set fire to his bed to make him get up. Sadly, the boy really was too ill to move.

Harold, the son of a caretaker, was kept chained in another room for 40 years. His mother would bring him food. People walking past heard Harold howling, and believed that the house was haunted. Harold's mother died. After some weeks, the townspeople found poor, starving Harold. He was put in a nursing home but died soon after.

Monte Cristo is now open as a tourist attraction. People can sleep over at the house. Guests often report seeing the ghost of Mrs. Crawley!

Bolsover Castle, England

Workmen working in the gardens at Bolsover Castle saw a woman in an old-fashioned dress disappear through a wall! Two of the workmen were so scared they refused to come back to work the next day. Many visitors say a Gray Lady walks on the grounds. Knights dressed in armor have also been seen in the garden.

A ghostly little boy is said to join any visiting children who play in the fountain garden. The boy has been seen trying to hold the children's hands.

THE FOUNTAIN GARDEN AND LITTLE CASTLE AT BOLSOVER

Bolsover Castle is now open to the public. Staff working there get so many reports of strange activity that they keep a "ghost book" for visitors to record their experiences! Most staff that work at the castle have experienced some kind of strange event.

The door to the old housekeeper's room sometimes won't open, as if it is locked. Ten minutes later it will open easily. Women have reported their legs have been touched in one of the bedrooms! One staff member felt a kick on her ankle in the **parlor** of the Little Castle. People have heard unexplained footsteps from the tower staircase. In the Well House, staff get a creepy feeling as if someone is watching them.

The Forbidden City, China

The Forbidden City in Beijing was home to Chinese royalty from 1420 to 1912. It was named the Forbidden City because no one could enter or leave without the emperor's permission! In 1421 Emperor Yongle ordered nearly 3,000 women living in the Forbidden City to be **slaughtered**. Visitors say they have seen a ghostly black-haired lady running from a phantom soldier.

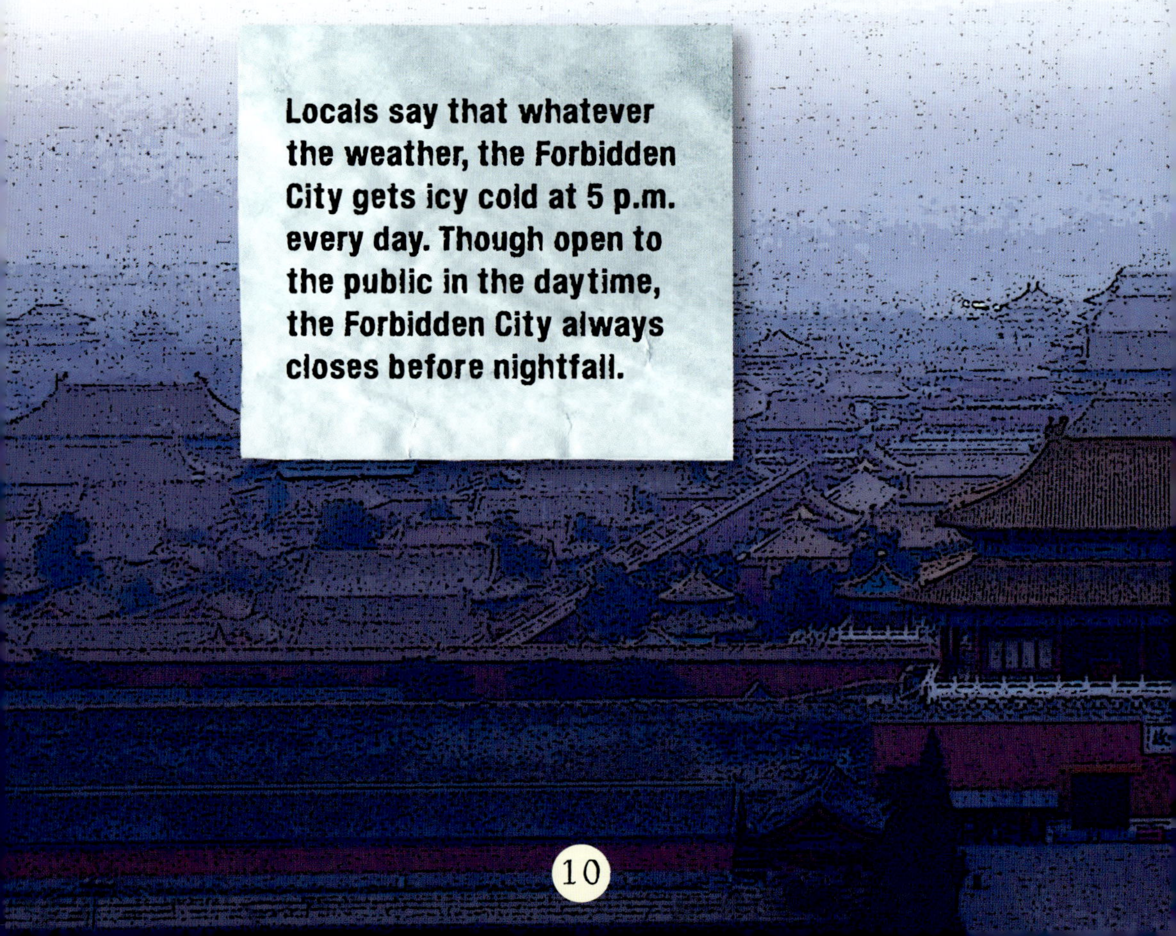

Locals say that whatever the weather, the Forbidden City gets icy cold at 5 p.m. every day. Though open to the public in the daytime, the Forbidden City always closes before nightfall.

Screams, weeping, and the sound of sword fighting are believed to be heard. Late at night, the palace guards have claimed to have seen ghostly bodies, scurrying animals, and mysterious pools of blood. In 1995, guards followed a woman they believed to be an intruder, but said that when she turned toward them, she had no face!

A woman is believed to have thrown herself down this well in the Forbidden City. If you dare look into it, her face is said to look back at you.

THE FORBIDDEN CITY AT NIGHTFALL

Borgvattnet Rectory, Sweden

When chaplain Nils Hedlund went up to the attic to fetch his laundry from the line, he says he watched as his clothes mysteriously flew to the floor. That was not the last time that ghosts have made their presence felt. Some years later, a priest named Rudolf Tangden saw an old woman in gray appear and vanish right in front of his eyes.

BORGVATTNET RECTORY

In 1945, chaplain Erik Lindgren experienced many strange things when he lived at the rectory. He was thrown out of his chair several times by an invisible force!

Erik Lindgren and his wife invited a friend to stay in their guest room. She said she woke in the night and saw three old women sitting on a couch staring at her! She turned on the light and the ladies began to blur. You can stay in the rectory if you dare. Guests receive a certificate if they manage to stay the whole night. Many leave in a hurry!

The Whaley House, San Diego

The Whaley House in San Diego has seen several tragic deaths and even a public hanging on the land. Perhaps it is not surprising that people have claimed to see ghosts there.

The Whaley House was the home of Thomas Whaley and his wife and six children. Here, the couple are pictured with two of the children.

Visitors to the house have reported seeing Thomas Whaley's ghost in the parlor (right). People have also heard the piano playing by itself!

"Yankee Jim" Robinson was hanged where the house now stands, after he was caught stealing. Thomas Whaley watched the **execution**, but still bought the land and built his house there. Soon after the Whaleys moved in, heavy footsteps were heard moving around the house. Whaley believed the footsteps were made by Yankee Jim.

Several children's spirits are said to haunt the house. People have heard a baby cry, and a young girl is said to grab visitors' arms! One of Whaley's sons, Thomas, died from illness at 18 months old. Whaley's great granddaughter died at the house after eating ant poison. A young playmate is also said to have broken her neck running into a clothesline while playing in the backyard.

THE WHALEY HOUSE

Rose Hall, Jamaica

This grand sugar **plantation** house in Montego Bay, Jamaica, was owned by the Palmer family. Local legend says that the lady of the house, Annie Palmer, murdered three of her husbands at Rose Hall. Annie was raised in Haiti and when her parents died she was adopted by a nanny who taught her **voodoo**. Voodoo is a religion from Haiti which uses a type of witchcraft.

Some believe that Annie Palmer haunts Rose Hall. However, historians have found no record of an Annie Palmer ever having lived there!

ROSE HALL

Cruel Annie Palmer is said to have **tortured** many of the plantation's slaves in this dark dungeon underneath the house. Whether Annie was real or not, slaves most certainly were kept there.

The story goes that Annie Palmer herself was murdered by a slave named Takoo. He murdered her because she had just murdered his niece. This tomb on the grounds is said to be her resting place.

Mohatta Palace, Pakistan

Indian **Hindu** businessman Shivratan Chandraratan Mohatta had the Mohatta Palace built as a summer home for his family. Built in 1927, the Mohatta family only enjoyed it for a few years. After Pakistan's independence from India in 1947, Mohatta left for India. The Pakistan government took over the palace. It lay empty for some years, and is now a museum.

Museum guards believe they have seen picture frames, flowerpots, sofas, and chairs move all by themselves. They also say they have heard noisy parties in the empty palace! Some believe the palace's long-dead owner may have returned.

Another legend that surrounds the palace is of an underground tunnel somewhere on the grounds. The tunnel is said to have been built to link the palace to an underground Hindu temple. The tunnel and temple were built for Mahatta's Hindu wife, so she could safely and privately worship. The tunnel is believed to still exist under the palace, but the entrance has been blocked off and long forgotten.

Château de Brissac, France

Early in the morning at the Château de Brissac, visitors sometimes hear terrible moans coming from the chapel. A double murder took place there, and the victims are said to haunt the house even today. Many people have reportedly seen the terrifying Green Lady.

The current Duke of Brissac and his family are used to seeing the ghost wandering around the house. Known as the Green Lady, she scares the Duke's guests whenever she appears!

She is usually seen in the tower room of the chapel, wearing a green dress. The most scary thing about her is that she has holes where her eyes and nose should be!

People have reported hearing strange moaning at the castle. Visitors have also heard the sound of a woman brushing her hair.

A past owner of the château, Jacques de Breze, thought his wife was too friendly with one of his **huntsmen**. He brutally stabbed her and the huntsman to death in the castle. Ever since the murders the home has been said to be haunted. Some have said they have seen the Green Lady screaming and grasping a knife stuck in her chest!

Castle of Good Hope, South Africa

Believed to be the most haunted place in South Africa, the Castle of Good Hope has a cruel history and apparently several ghosts. In the 1700s, a soldier was found hanging dead from a rope in the bell tower. The tower was sealed off so this could not happen again. The bell is sometimes still heard to strike, even though no one is in the tower!

THE BELL TOWER AT THE CASTLE OF GOOD HOPE

Many prisoners were tortured in the castle dungeons. Built on the coast, at **high tide** the seawater moat would sometimes flood the underground dungeon, drowning the chained prisoners.

A lady in a gray hood has been seen running through the castle, crying and holding her face. The same ghostly lady has been spotted in one of the bedrooms at the castle. She was seen at the foot of the bed with her head in her hands, but then she faded and disappeared.

Moosham Castle, Austria

The ancient castle at Moosham, Austria, has a sinister past. Over one hundred suspected witches were **beheaded** within the walls of the castle. Some people believe that they still haunt the fortress today.

Many thousands were accused of witchcraft. Men, women, and even children who were accused were tortured at the castle. Any that confessed were killed. After all that suffering within its walls, it is not surprising the castle feels creepy.

In the torture chamber, visitors claim they have felt hands touch their hair and legs. Others have said they feel as if someone is breathing on them. Banging sounds and footsteps have been heard at the castle. Doors sometimes slam shut for no reason. Voices and screams have also been heard!

In the 1800s there was a rumor **werewolves** lived in the castle. Livestock had been found gored to death. People accused of being werewolves were taken prisoner or executed!

A WEREWOLF

Charleville Castle, Ireland

Charleville Castle is said to be the most haunted building in Europe. Many of the ghosts are said to be of children. In the early morning people have been woken by the sound of children playing in the nursery. The daughter of a recent owner was even found locked in a cupboard in her playroom by an unknown presence!

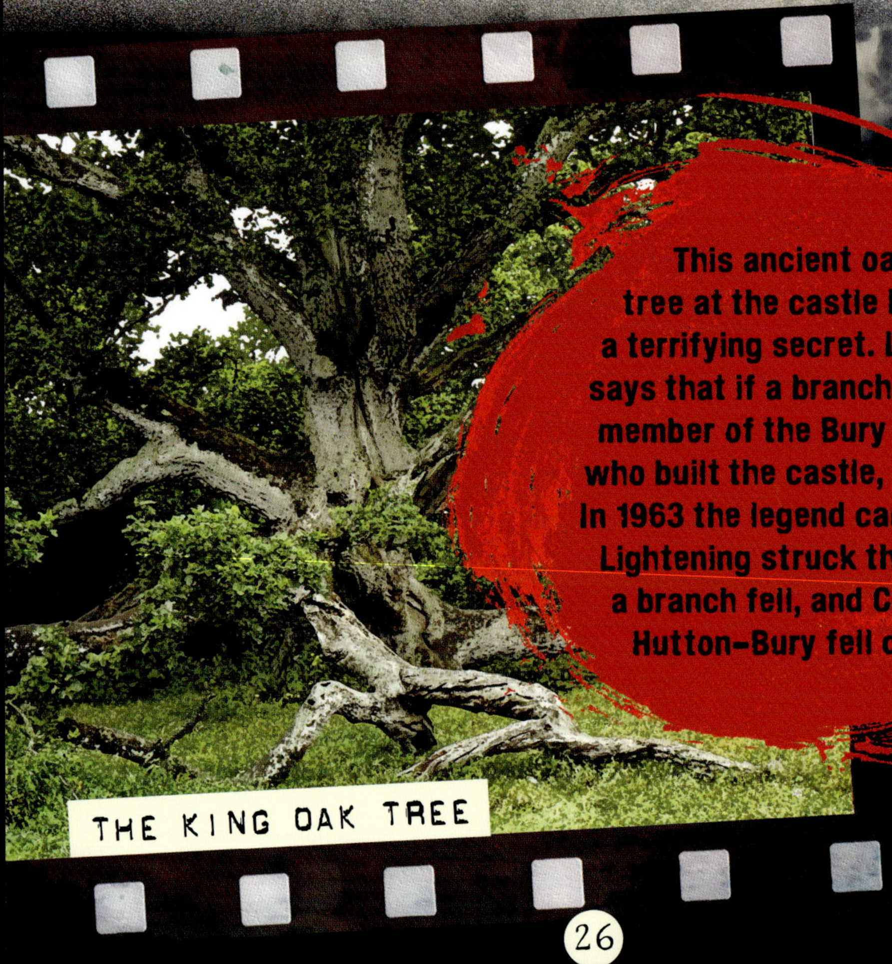

This ancient oak tree at the castle holds a terrifying secret. Legend says that if a branch falls, a member of the Bury family, who built the castle, will die! In 1963 the legend came true. Lightening struck the tree, a branch fell, and Charles Hutton-Bury fell dead!

THE KING OAK TREE

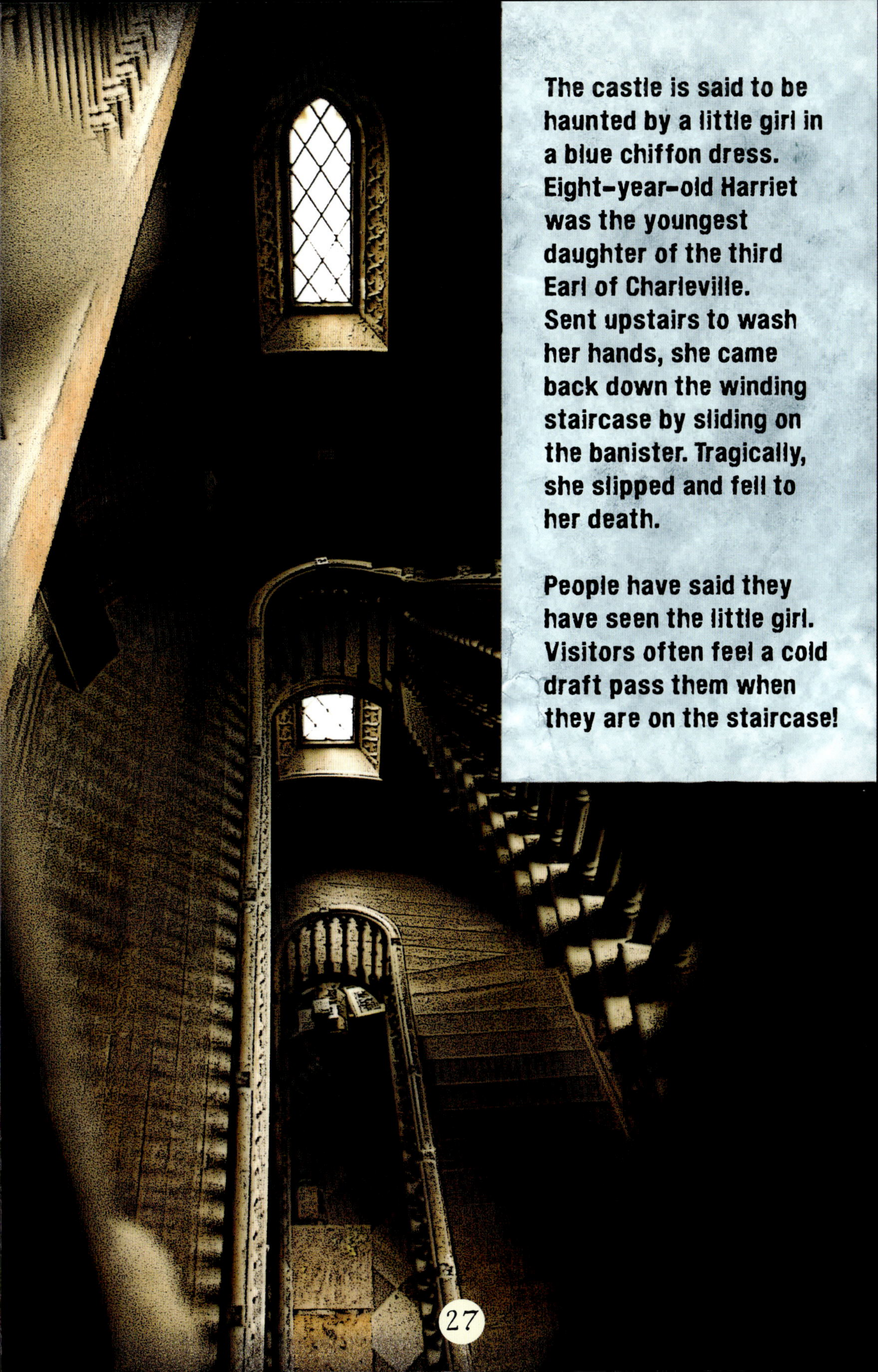

The castle is said to be haunted by a little girl in a blue chiffon dress. Eight-year-old Harriet was the youngest daughter of the third Earl of Charleville. Sent upstairs to wash her hands, she came back down the winding staircase by sliding on the banister. Tragically, she slipped and fell to her death.

People have said they have seen the little girl. Visitors often feel a cold draft pass them when they are on the staircase!

The White House, Washington, DC

With so much history having taken place at the White House, perhaps it's not surprising that the house is thought to be haunted. Past presidents Abraham Lincoln, Theodore Roosevelt, Herbert Hoover, Dwight Eisenhower, Andrew Jackson, John Tyler, and Thomas Jefferson are all believed to have been seen wandering around the house! Cold spots, footsteps, voices, screams, and knocking noises have been heard, as well as loud laughing and arguing!

THE LINCOLN BEDROOM

While staying in the Lincoln Bedroom, British Prime Minister Winston Churchill said he once saw Abraham Lincoln (below) standing by the fireplace. He refused to ever sleep in that room again!

Glossary

atmosphere The mood of a place.

beheaded Had the head cut off.

execution A putting to death as a punishment.

haunt To visit or live in as a ghost.

high tide The tide when the water is at its greatest height.

Hindu A follower of a religion from India.

huntsmen People who hunt game.

nanny A person, typically a woman, employed to look after a child in its own home.

parlor A room for receiving and talking with guests.

plantation An agricultural estate worked by laborers.

slaughtered Killed without mercy or in large numbers.

tortured To punish or force someone to do or say something by causing great pain.

voodoo A religion that is based on African ancestor worship and practiced chiefly in Haiti.

werewolves People who changed or were able to change into a wolf.

Further Information

McCollum, Sean. *Paranormal Handbook to Ghosts, Poltergeists, and Haunted Houses.* Mankato, MN: Raintree, 2016.

Owings, Lisa. *Ghosts in the White House (Ghost Stories).* Las Vegas, NV: Epic, 2016.

Website

Ducksters biography of Abraham Lincoln:
www.ducksters.com/biography/uspresidents/abrahamlincoln.php

Publisher's note to educators and parents:
Our editors have carefully reviewed these websites to ensure that they are suitable for students. Many websites change frequently, however, and we cannot guarantee that a site's future contents will continue to meet our high standards of quality and educational value. Be advised that students should be closely supervised whenever they access the Internet.

Index

Don't be scared! Most people don't believe ghosts are real at all. No one has ever scientifically proven they exist. But it can be fun to get yourself a little spooked!